Jet Attack

Janice Pimm • Jon Stuart

Contents

D1420121

OXFORD

UNIVERSITY PRESS

Macro Marvel
(billionaire inventor)

Welcome to Micro World!

Macro Marvel invented Micro World – a micro-sized theme park where you have to shrink to get in.

A computer called *CODE* controls Micro World and all the robots inside – MITEs and BITEs.

A MITE

A BITE

Disaster strikes!

CODE goes wrong on opening day.
CODE wants to shrink the world.

Macro Marvel is trapped inside the park …

Enter Team X!

Four micro agents – **Max, Cat, Ant** and **Tiger** – are sent to rescue Macro Marvel and defeat CODE.

Mini Marvel joins Team X.

Mini Marvel
(Macro's daughter)

Together they have to:

- Defeat the BITEs
- Collect the CODE keys
- Rescue Macro Marvel
- Stop CODE
- Save the world!

**CODE key
(1 collected)**

Look at the map on page 4. You are in the Galactic Orbit zone.

Before you read

Sound checker
Say the sounds.

oo   **oa**

Sound spotter
Blend the sounds.

| m | oo | n |

| l | oo | k |

| f | l | oa | t | i | ng |

| r | oa | s | t | i | ng |

Tricky words

are
they
all

Into the zone

What do you think the ride
in this zone will be like?

On the Rocket

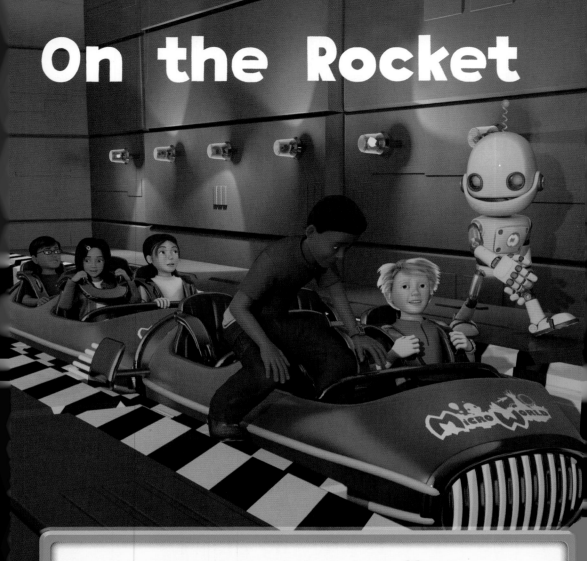

Team X and Mini are off on a quest.
They jump in the rocket.
The MITE checks they are all right.

moon

The rocket zooms up and up to the moon.
It swoops fast.
Hang on tight, Team X!

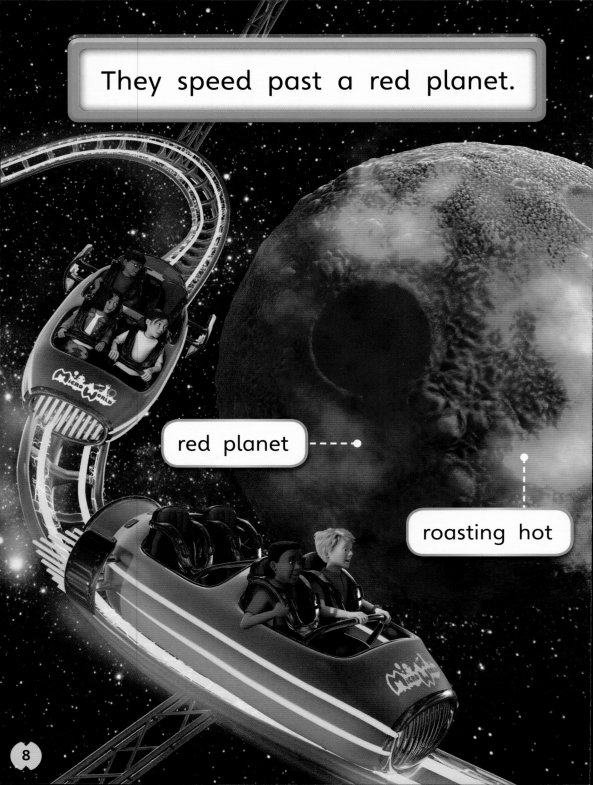

They speed past a red planet.

red planet

roasting hot

Look!

They loop the loop.
Look! Is that a jet?
Is it the BITE?

floating moon

green planet

dust

Off they go into the black night.

Now you have read ...
On the Rocket

Text checker

Read the words that describe how the ride moves.
Which words would you use to describe this picture?

zooms

swoops

loop the loop

MITE fun

Look carefully at the picture of the rocket ride.
Close your eyes and imagine what it would be
like to go on this ride. Now describe the ride to
someone else.

I like the
rocket ride!

Before you read

Sound checker
Say the sounds.

oo   oa

Sound spotter
Blend the sounds.

r	oa	d

l	oo	k

v	r	oo	m

Tricky words
they
you
was
are

Into the zone
What might happen to
Team X and Mini on
the green planet?

12

Planet of Doom

Green Planet

The rocket stops.
Is the CODE key on this planet?
Max and Tiger go to look.

They look on the road and under a rock.

They look in the green dust but
they can not see the CODE key.

What is that? Tiger jumps.
It is a jet!

The jet swoops at Max and Tiger.

Max and Tiger run but the jet swoops again.

Tiger can see into the jet.
It is the BITE!

Then the wind blows the dust.
The jet might crash!
It zooms off!

I will be back!

That was lucky!

Max and Tiger can not see the road.
Thud! They land in a pit.

Max and Tiger are stuck.
What can they do?

Now you have read ...
Planet of Doom

Text checker
What made Tiger jump?

MITE fun
Max and Tiger do not agree about the green dust cloud.
Was it good or bad? Finish the sentences.

The dust cloud was good because ...

The dust cloud was bad because ...

What do you think my name is?